Jags for

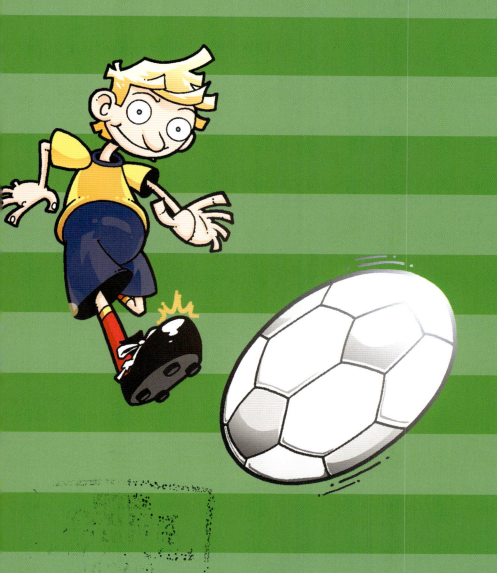

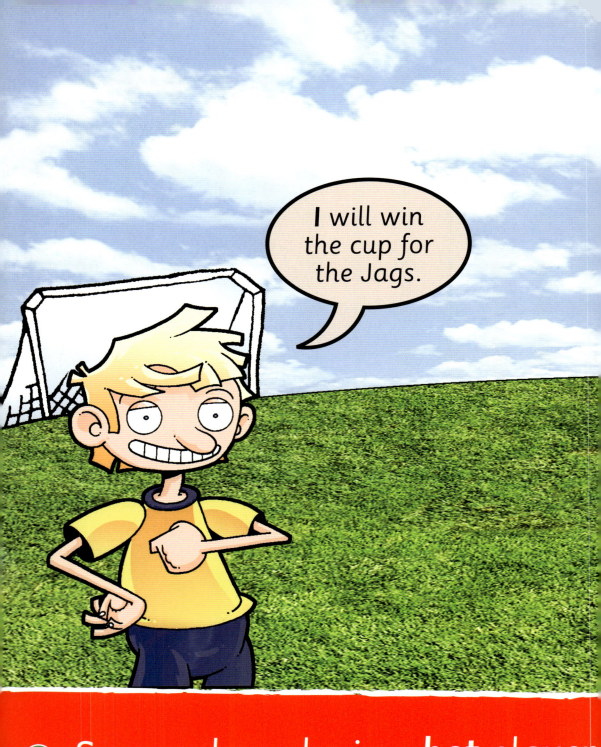

4 Sam reckons he is a **hot** player

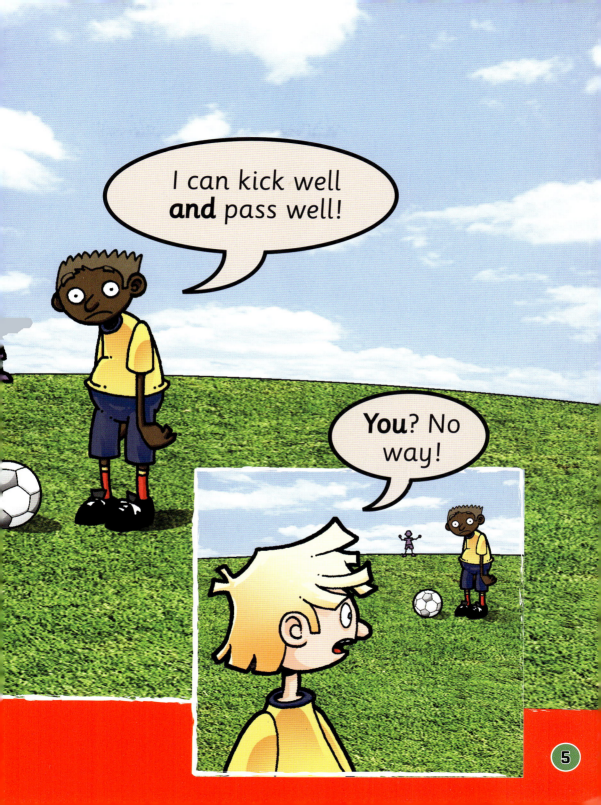

Dan gets fit for the match.

He huffs and he puffs!

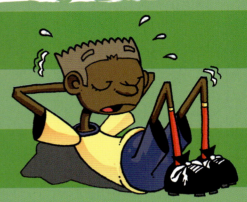

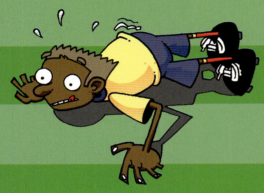

He jogs and he runs.

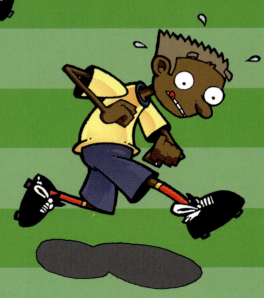

But not Sam. He pigs out.

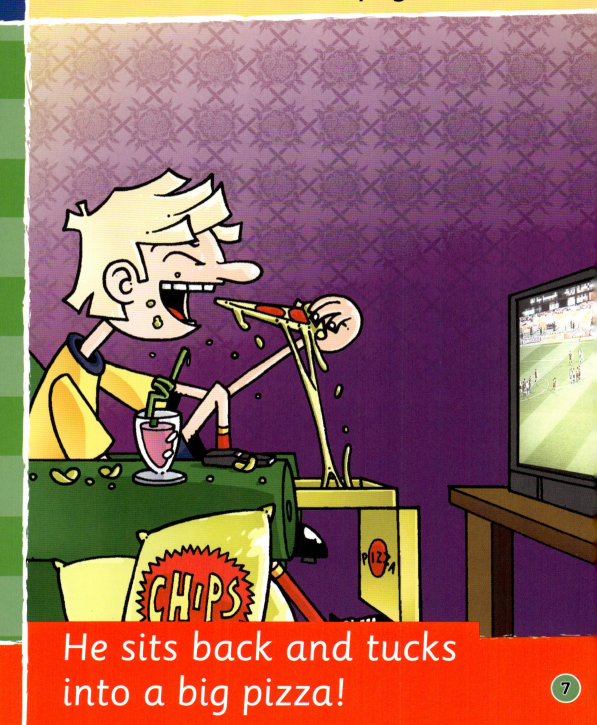

He sits back and tucks into a big pizza!

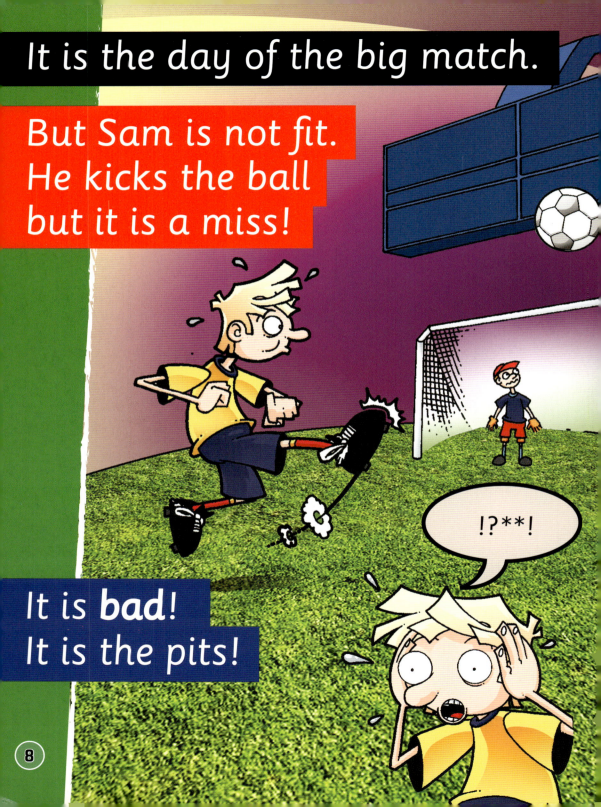

But not Dan! He pops up in the box and …

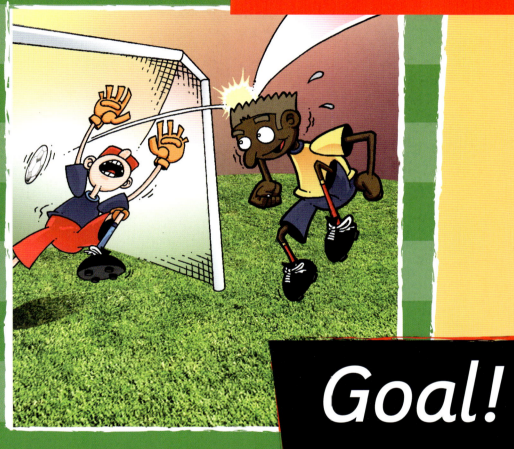

Goal!

It is in the net.

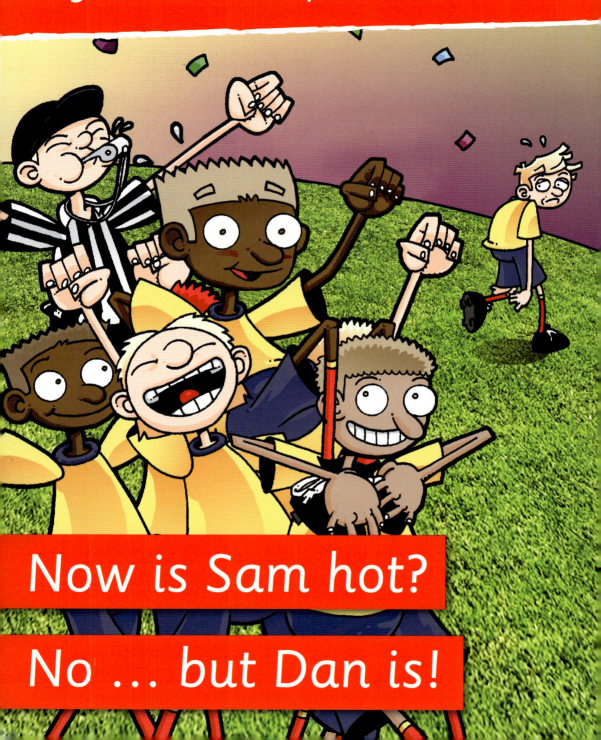